CHARTING YOUR COURSE

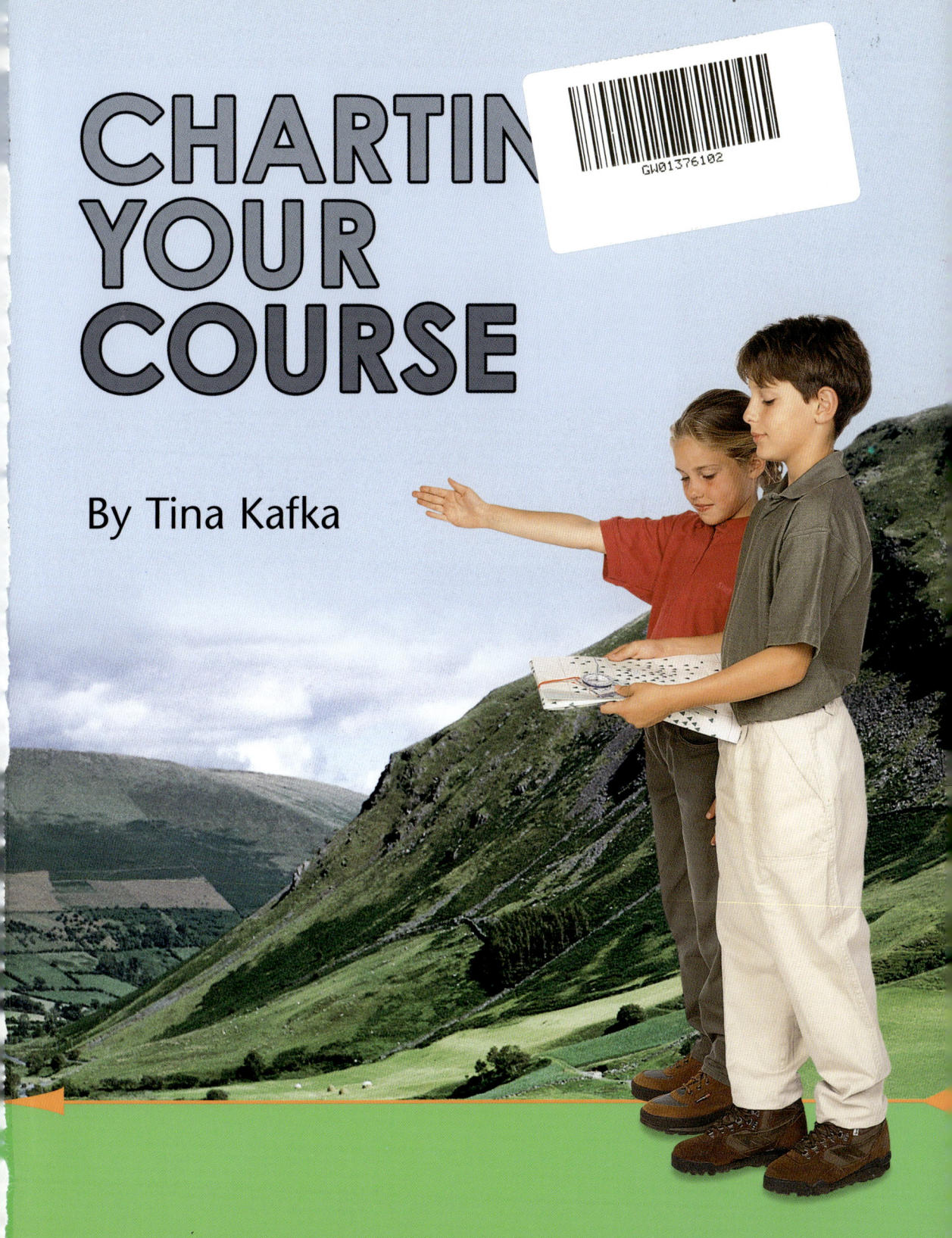

By Tina Kafka

Contents

Get Ready to Explore 3

Measuring Weather 4
    Use a Thermometer 5
    How to Make a Thermometer 6
    Use a Barometer 9
    How to Read a Barometer 10
    Charting the Weather 12

Things to Take With You 14
    How to Read a Compass 15
    How to Make a Compass 17
    How to Make a Periscope 20

Adventure Awaits 23

Glossary 24

Get Ready to Explore

Do you like exploring city parks or camping outdoors? Do you like hiking? If so, this guide will help you make the most of your outdoor adventures.

You will learn how to make useful tools. Some of these tools will help you measure changes in the **weather**. Other tools will help you find your way. Before you set out on your next adventure, be prepared. Remember to tell an adult where you plan to go, or ask an adult to join in the fun, too.

Measuring Weather

How much fun we have outdoors depends on the **weather**. Scientists who study the weather are called **meteorologists**. They use different instruments to measure and predict changes in the **weather**. They use **thermometers** to measure changes in temperature and **barometers** to measure **air pressure**. You, too, can learn how to study the weather.

Meteorologists forecast, or make predictions about, the weather.

Use a Thermometer

Before you go on a trip, always check the temperature. Then you'll know what type of clothes to wear or take with you. You will learn how to make a simple thermometer on pages 6–7. Your homemade thermometer will show changes in the temperature from day to day. Use it with a shop-bought thermometer to find the exact temperature in **degrees**.

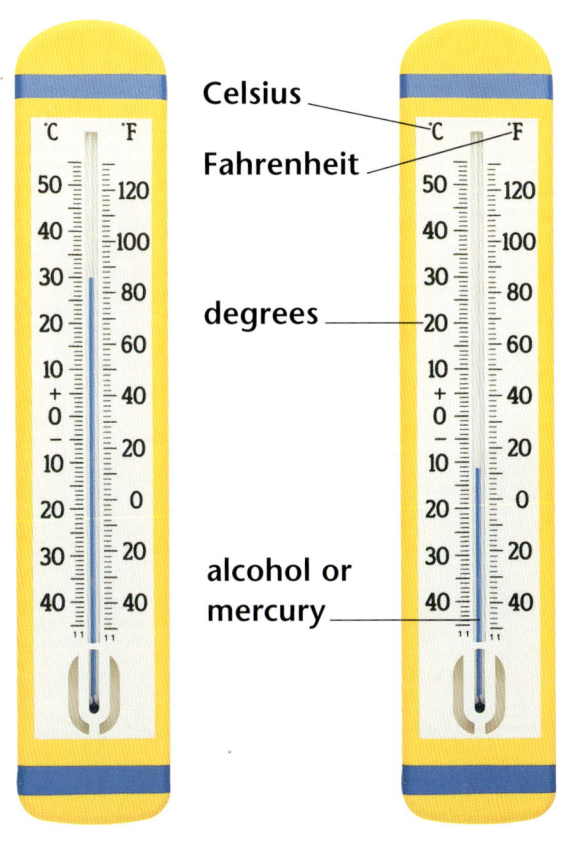

Celsius
Fahrenheit
degrees
alcohol or mercury

high temperature   low temperature

When the air gets warmer, the liquid in a thermometer moves up the tube. When the air gets cooler, the liquid moves down the tube.

! Safety With Mercury

The liquid inside some thermometers, mercury, is very dangerous. Never touch or breathe in mercury. If mercury leaks or spills from your thermometer, stand back and call an adult immediately.

How to Make a Thermometer

Materials

- a small glass bottle
- cold water
- food colouring
- a clear straw
- modelling clay
- scissors
- 5-by-8 cm strip of paper
- red and black marker pens
- a shop-bought thermometer

Procedure

1 Fill the bottle about two-thirds full with cold water. Then add a few drops of food colouring.

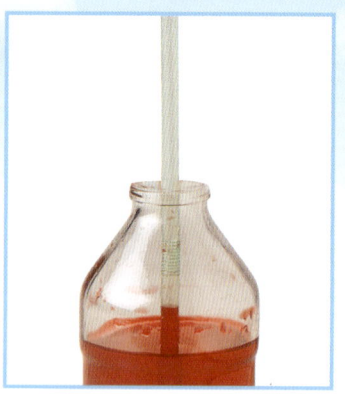

2 Put the straw into the bottle so that its tip dips into the water.

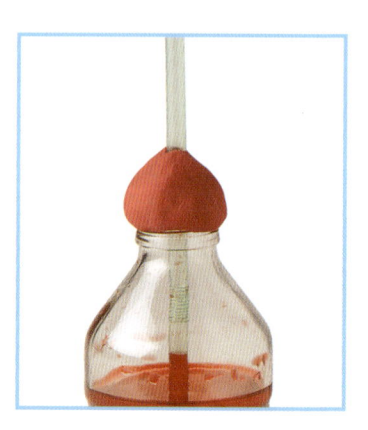

3 Tuck some clay around the straw in the bottle's opening to keep the straw in place.

4 Blow air gently into the straw until, when you stop blowing, the water rises about halfway up the straw.

5 Fold the strip of paper in half and cut four slits. Unfold the paper and slide it over the straw.

6 Make a black mark on the paper next to the water level. Check the temperature on the shop-bought thermometer and write it near the black mark.

7 Place your homemade thermometer and the shop-bought thermometer in a warm place. Leave them there for 30 to 60 minutes.

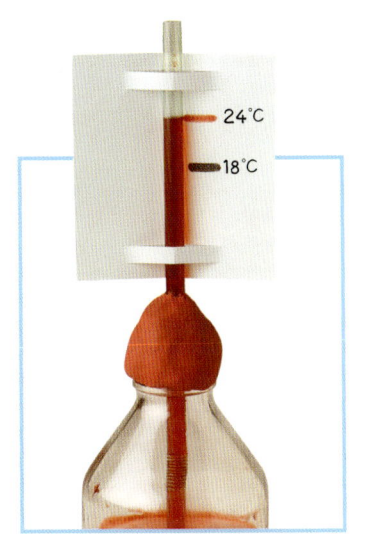

8 Mark the water level in red and write the temperature number by it, as you did in Step 6.

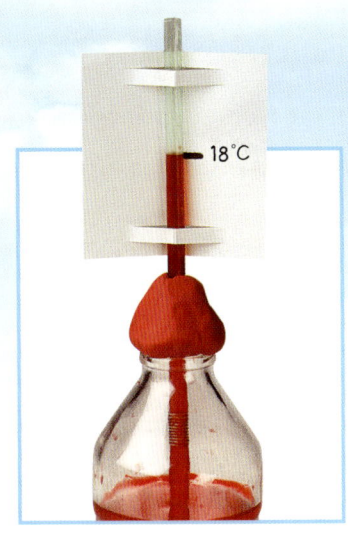

9 Place the two thermometers in a cold place. Wait 30 to 60 minutes. Mark the water level in blue and write the temperature.

Top Tips

Here are hot and cold places where you can try out your thermometer:

- on a sunny windowsill
- beside a heater
- in a shed or garage
- in a fridge
- in a greenhouse

Temperature Measurements

Thermometers measure the **temperature** in degrees. Anders Celsius was a Swedish astronomer. The Celsius temperature scale was named after him. The Celsius scale is also called the centigrade scale because it is divided into 100 degrees. Daniel Gabriel Fahrenheit invented the mercury thermometer in 1714. The Fahrenheit scale was named after him.

Think About It

What causes the water to move in the straw in your homemade thermometer? If you measure the air temperature in different places inside and outside your home or school, how does it change? Remember to let the thermometer sit in each place for at least 30 minutes.

Use your homemade thermometer in places where the temperature is above 0°C. Water freezes at 0°C, which could cause the thermometer to break.

Use a Barometer

Before you go on a trip, find out if the **weather** will be sunny or cloudy. A **barometer** helps predict the weather. It measures **air pressure**, which is the weight of air pressing down on the Earth.

You will learn how to read a barometer on page 10. Then you will be able to tell when there will be fair or rainy weather.

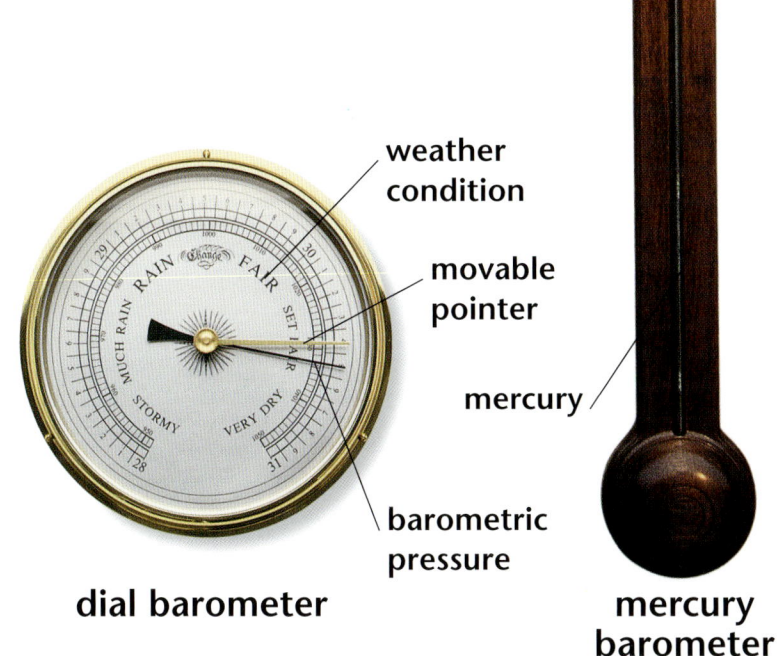

How Heavy Is Air?

All around the Earth is a layer of air that is several kilometres thick. It is made up of gases we can't see. Although air is invisible, it still has weight. All of the air around the Earth weighs about 5 **quadrillion** tonnes!

- weather condition
- movable pointer
- mercury
- barometric pressure

dial barometer

mercury barometer

Earth's atmosphere as seen from space

9

How to Read a Barometer

There are different types of **barometer**. Two types that people might have at home are the water barometer and the dial barometer.

A water barometer is read by noting changes in how high or low the water rises in the tube. Low pressure causes the water level to rise. High pressure causes the water level to go down.

water barometer

Materials

- a shop-bought water barometer and a dial barometer

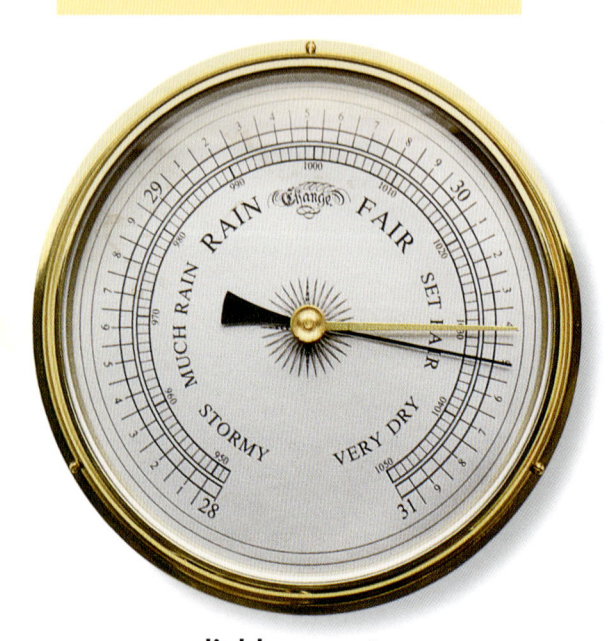

Procedure

1. Listen to your local **weather** forecast to find out what the **air pressure** is for your area on a clear day. Use this number to mark a starting point on the water barometer. This number should be the same as on the dial barometer.

2. Find the black pointer or needle on the dial barometer. Then read the numbers around the edge of the dial. The needle should be pointing to a number between 28 and 31. This is the air pressure.

dial barometer

How Barometers Were Invented

An Italian scientist called Evangelista Torricelli invented the barometer in the 1640s. At first, Torricelli used water in a tube closed at the top. Then he changed to mercury. He saw that the height of the mercury in the tube changed from day to day. He discovered that this happened because of changes in air pressure.

This barometer reads "Very Dry", predicting fair weather.

This barometer reads "Rain", predicting poor weather.

Evangelista Torricelli

Think About It

Why do the barometer's readings vary? What does your barometer do when a storm threatens?

Weather Symbols

sun

rain

wind

hail

thunder

some clouds

snow

clouds

Charting the Weather

Make a **weather** chart to see how changes in temperature and air pressure affect the weather. Record each day's temperature, **air pressure** and weather conditions. After a week or two, compare the data.

Materials

- a thermometer
- a barometer
- a large sheet of paper
- coloured marker pens
- a ruler

Procedure

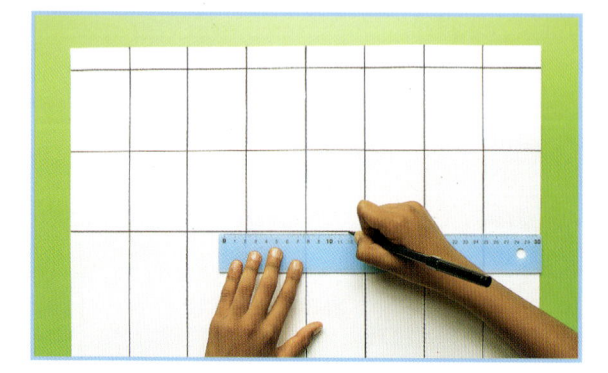

1 Decide on the number of days you plan to observe the weather. Draw this number of columns plus one more. Then draw four rows across the sheet of paper.

2 Make up your own symbols to show the weather conditions, or use the ones shown on page 12. Weather conditions could include sunny, rainy, cloudy, snowy and windy.

3 Observe the weather each day. Record the type of weather on the chart.

4 Place the thermometer and barometer in a safe place outside. Observe the temperature and barometer readings each day, and record them on the chart.

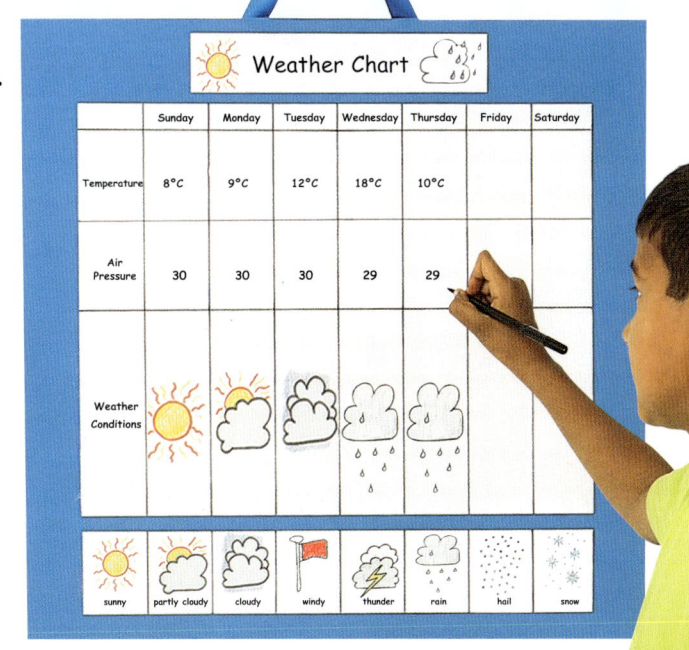

Think About It

When you look at your weather chart, what changes do you see? Did the temperature or air pressure change before the weather changed? How would these changes help you to forecast the weather?

Things to Take With You

Before going on a trip, you need to know the direction you want to travel. Are you going to go north, south, east or west? Use a **compass** to help you find your way. In this section, you'll learn how easy it is to use a compass. You will learn how to make a compass on pages 17–18.

Use a **periscope** when you go on a trip. A periscope is a long tube with a mirror at each end. Periscopes help you to look over high objects and around corners. You will learn how to make a periscope on pages 20–21.

These people are using periscopes to look over the heads of people in a crowd.

How to Use a Compass

Materials

- a shop-bought compass

compass point

needle

degrees

dial

Procedure

1 First find the letters N, E, S and W around the dial or the edge of the compass. The letters stand for north, east, south and west.

2 Then find the needle that spins in the middle of the compass. This is a **magnet** that always points towards north and south. One half of the needle is either red or marked with an N to show north. Now, find the north point of the needle.

How Does a Compass Work?

On a compass, only the needle is a magnet. One end of a compass needle always points north. The other end points south. By lining up the needle with the N on the dial, you can work out which way is north, south, east and west.

15

direction line

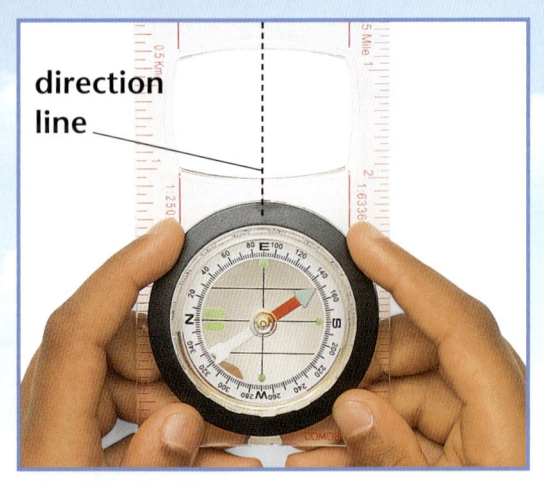

3 Find the direction line or arrow. In some **compasses** this line lies outside the dial. Next, turn the dial so that the direction in which you want to go, such as E, lines up with the direction line.

4 Hold the compass steady in your hand and keep away from metal objects. Metal objects may be magnetic, which will affect the needle's accuracy.

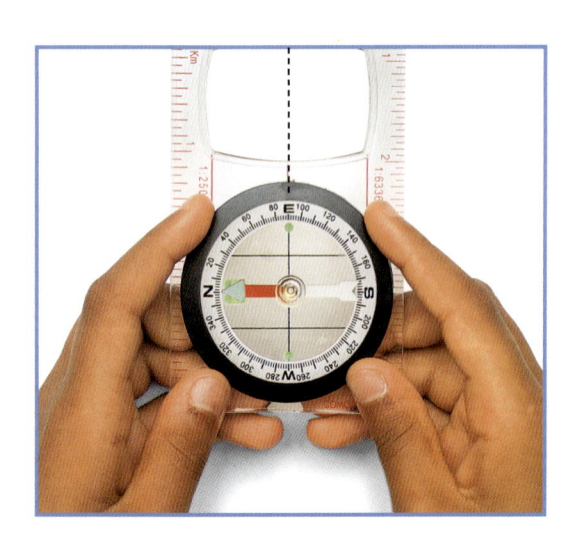

5 Turn yourself so that the north end of the needle points towards the N on the compass dial. The direction line now shows in which direction you should walk.

6 If your compass does not have a dial that turns or a direction arrow, hold the compass in front of you. Turn yourself around until the north end of the needle lines up with the N on the compass face.

How to Make a Compass

Now that you know how to read a compass, you're ready to make one of your own. You will need a small **magnet**. If you always have a magnet with you when you explore, you may be able to find the other materials needed to make a compass almost anywhere.

Top Tips

When you magnetize a piece of metal, such as a needle, it will only stay magnetic for a short time. A magnet may become **demagnetized** if the needle gets hot or is dropped. If this happens, just magnetize the needle again.

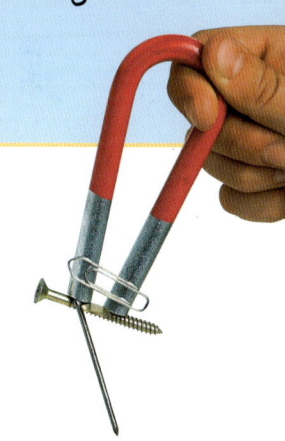

Materials

- a magnet
- a sewing needle
- tape
- a piece of cork
- a small bowl of water
- a marker pen
- a shop-bought compass

Procedure

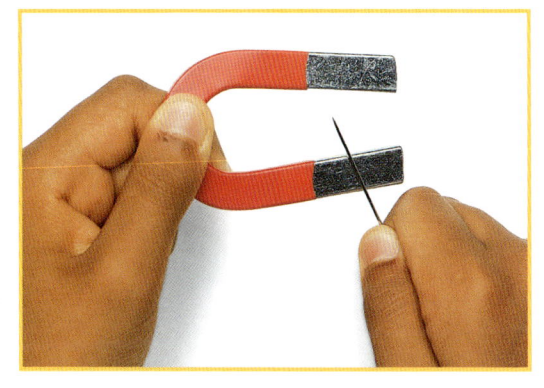

1 Rub one pole of the magnet up and down the needle. Repeat this about thirty times.

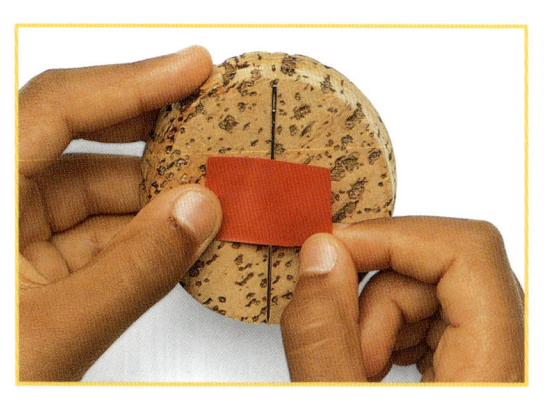

2 Tape the needle to the middle of the cork.

3 Float the cork in the bowl of water. The cork will move so that the needle points north and south. Use your shop-bought compass to see which direction is north.

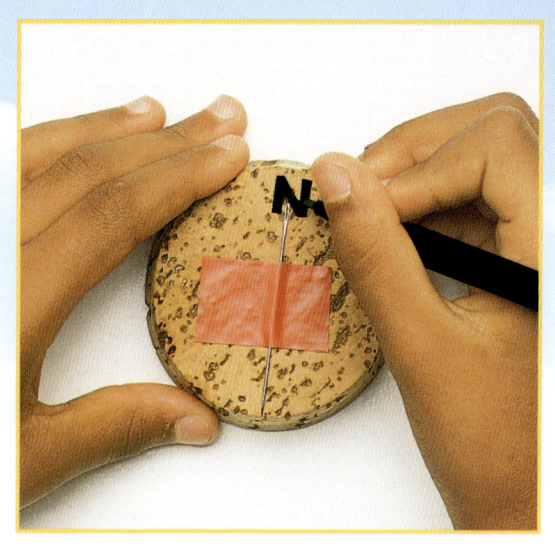

4 Mark the cork with an *N* so you can tell which end of the needle points north.

5 Mark south on the cork. (South is opposite north on the other half of the cork.) Then mark east and west with an *E* and *W*.

6 Use your homemade compass to find directions at school or at home.

18

Safety With Compasses

A homemade compass is good to use inside your home or at school. However, if you go outside or on a trip, then always go with a teacher or other adult and use a shop-bought compass.

Practise using your compass outside. Walk for a few minutes keeping the compass level and steady, then stop and get your bearings. Change direction and walk for a few more minutes. Stop and get your bearings again. Repeat this activity a few times. Soon you'll be a compass expert.

Think About It

Why is it important that the compass be kept level and steady? How would you use the compass to find the north side of your school's playground? How would you use it to find the direction your desk faces in the classroom?

How Does a Periscope Work?

A **periscope** uses two mirrors that are tilted. This allows light to reflect from the top mirror down to the bottom mirror. From there it reflects to the person's eye.

How to Make a Periscope

Materials

- a small cardboard triangle
- a tall empty milk or fruit juice carton
- scissors
- a sharp pencil
- a ruler
- two small mirrors, a little wider than the carton

Ask an adult to help you with this activity.

Procedure

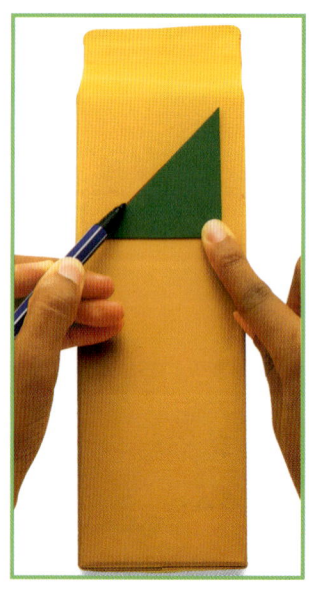

1 Use a cardboard triangle to help you draw two parallel, diagonal lines. One line should be near the top of the carton and the other near the bottom.

2 Carefully cut a slot along each line that is just wide enough for a mirror to fit through.

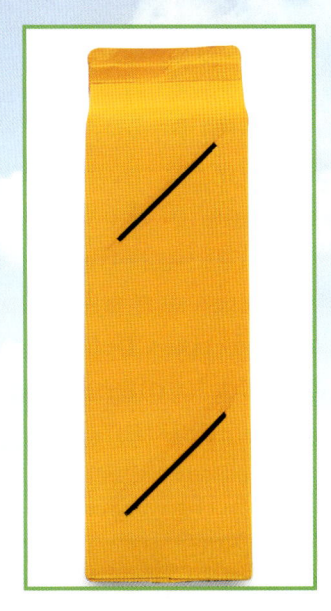

3 Turn the carton and draw two lines on the other side, directly opposite the slots you have already cut. Cut slots along these lines, too.

4 Carefully push the mirrors into the slots. They should face each other (top mirror facing down, bottom mirror facing up) and fit snugly.

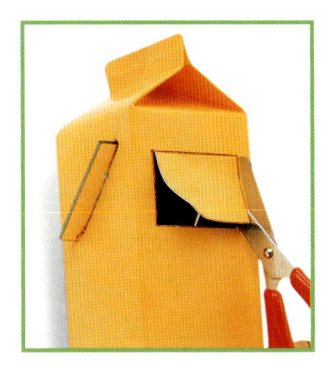

5 Draw a large square at the top of the carton in front of the top mirror. Carefully cut out the square.

6 Make a small hole with a pencil in the back of your periscope. The hole should be level with the bottom mirror.

21

Periscopes

Periscopes can be different lengths. The longer the periscope, the smaller the image seen through the eyehole. Periscopes in submarines have **lenses** between the mirrors to magnify the image, making it look closer and larger.

Now you're ready to peer around corners and see over walls. Practise using your **periscope** around the house. See how useful a periscope can be.

Think About It

When would it be very difficult to use a periscope to see things? How could you make a periscope so that you could see what was behind you?

Adventure Awaits

Now you know how to make and use some of the tools that every explorer needs. You're ready to plan your next adventure with the help of an adult. You know how to check the **weather** before you leave. You can use a **compass** to stay on course. You also have a periscope to make exploring more fun. Why not teach a friend what you've learned and go together on your next adventure?

Glossary

air pressure	the force with which air presses down on the Earth and on everything in the atmosphere
barometers	instruments that measure air pressure
compass	an instrument that shows where north is
degrees	units of measure
demagnetized	loss of the ability to attract iron and some other metals
lenses	pieces of glass or plastic curved on one or both sides that make objects appear larger or smaller
magnet	a metal that attracts iron and some other metals
meteorologists	scientists who study the weather
periscope	an instrument for seeing things that are not directly in sight
quadrillion	1,000,000,000,000,000
thermometers	instruments that measure temperature
weather	the conditions outside, such as temperature, sunshine and rain